FIFTY-TWO
INVITATION
ILLUSTRATIONS

by Billy Apostolon

BAKER BOOK HOUSE
Grand Rapids, Michigan

DEDICATION

This book is dedicated to
UNCLE JOE AND AUNT WANDA HONAKER
faithful Christian friends through the years of our ministry
who have served the Lord and His people faithfully
with the desire to see the Lord's will accomplished
and who have helped this author and his family
exceedingly much more than our words can express.
Mark 14:9

ISBN: 0-8010-0041-6

Copyright, 1972, by
Baker Book House Company

Fourth printing, February 1978

PRINTED IN THE UNITED STATES OF AMERICA

FOREWORD

The reception of *Fifty-two Evangelistic Illustrations* and *Fifty-two Soul-Stirring Illustrations* reveals the need for this third volume.

It has been a joy for this author to collect these illustrations during the years of his busy ministry. Since the Christian life is a life of sharing, it is this writer's desire to share these illustrations with other ministers who may not have the time nor the source to secure illustrations for themselves.

These illustrations have been gleaned from the writings of the great preachers of the world who have lived in the past generations and those who live in the present. Some have been chosen from the sermons of these men while others have been chosen from various other writings. Whenever possible we have listed the author which will make the illustrations more useful to those who use them. We are exceedingly grateful to the various sources from which the illustrations which make up this book are taken.

These fifty-two illustrations in this book were specifically chosen to be used just before the singing of the invitation hymn. Each has an evangelistic appeal designed to stir individuals to make a spiritual decision for the Lord Jesus Christ. Here the minister of God's Word will find illustrations for fifty-two Sunday evangelistic services or fifty-two other evangelistic services. We have given titles to each illustration which we believe will be helpful to the user in choosing the proper illustration for each occasion.

These illustrations are sent forth with the prayer of the author that they may be used to enlighten individuals and encourage them to receive the Lord Jesus Christ as their personal Saviour. If this is accomplished then the labor of love spent in preparing this book will be well spent and the Lord Jesus shall have all the glory for this work which is sent forth in His Precious Name.

Billy Apostolon

Hinton, West Virginia
1972

Contents

1. The Deacon Who Won Himself to the Lord

Our Lord Jesus Christ said:

"Not every one that saith unto me, Lord, Lord, shall enter into the kingdom of heaven; but he that doeth the will of my father which is in heaven.

Many will say to me in that day, Lord, Lord, have we not prophesied in thy name? and in thy name have cast out devils? and in thy name done many wonderful works?

And then will I profess unto them, I never knew you: depart from me, ye that work iniquity" (Matt. 7:21-23).

It is a tragedy that many who are church members and who hold offices in churches have never been born again. However, it is a blessing when those who have been church members and have held offices in churches recognize that they have not been born again and are lost and receive the Lord Jesus Christ as their personal Saviour.

Jack Hyles, pastor of the First Baptist Church of Hammond, Indiana tells of such an incident. Dr. Hyles said:

"For many years I have trained the deacons of the churches I have pastored to do the personal soul winning at the altar during the invitation time. As the people come forward to receive Christ as Saviour, the deacons also come forward to deal with them. I will simply say to a deacon, 'This man wants to receive Christ as Saviour, would you kneel and pray with him please.' The deacon takes his Bible, opens it, kneels at the altar with the seeker, presents the plan of salvation to him, and leads him to a saving knowledge of Christ.

"Once I went through this normal procedure only to have the deacon jump to his feet and come to me speaking in an excited voice saying, 'Preacher, I won myself to Christ! I won myself to Christ! I won myself to Christ!' I inquired as to the meaning of his statement. He then told me that for years he had known the plan of salvation but had never been born again. He related how that upon kneeling at the altar, presenting the plan to the seeker, he himself prayed the sinner's prayer and placed his faith in the finished work of Calvary. Yes, he had won himself to Christ, as he won another."

Are you a lost church member? If you are, won't you follow the example of this deacon and receive the Lord Jesus Christ as your personal Saviour?

The Lord Jesus said: ". . . Verily, verily, I say unto thee, Except a man be born again, he cannot see the kingdom of God" (John 3:3).

—Billy Apostolon,
Minister, Author, Educator, Hinton, West Virginia

2. The Folly of Rejecting Jesus Christ

There is an old story written in history books and one which reveals the tragedy of the Conemaugh Valley, the Conemaugh Dam. The engineers were sent to the valley. They checked the dam and said it was going to break. They pointed out certain weaknesses that made the dam unsafe. After they made their investigation, the engineers rode down the valley, and began to warn the people saying, "Move out! Get on higher ground! Get rid of everything and get away from the danger!"

The engineers went away and the people remained. Then the engineers returned a second time. They checked the dam again. Then they warned the people again, urging them to move before the dam broke and the entire valley flooded. This time the folks laughed. They said, "You were here a short time ago and nothing has happened. Everything is just as it was."

The engineers again went on their way, knowing that they had done their best. Then for a third time they came back— this was in the spring of the year. This time their warning was more urgent. They told every man, every woman, every child, everyone, "You must get out at once! Move out of here! Get to a higher place! To a safer place!"

The people again scorned their warning. "You are trying to

get our land. This is rich and good land, and we are not going to move."

The engineers rode out of the valley. In fifteen days' time there came a man riding swiftly, on horseback as in the olden days, crying as he rode, "The waters are coming! The dam is breaking! The waters are coming!" He kept on shouting and screaming and crying, and still, they tell us, some people stood and laughed at him!

He was not out of their sight before they could hear the sound of the waters, for the Conemaugh Dam had broken, and in just a few minutes thirty-three hundred people had lost their lives. It took over six weeks to dig their bodies out of the refuse, the muck and the mire.

Listen! They had been warned, not once, not twice, but three times, even as I am seeking to warn you today to turn to Jesus Christ, to repent and believe, and receive Him as your Saviour.

—Lee Roberson, President-Founder of Tennessee Temple Schools, and pastor of Highland Park Baptist Church, Chattanooga, Tennessee.

3. The Power of Heaven for Salvation

Several radio listeners asked me what the click is they hear occasionally as I am preaching. It is the switch of a light on my desk. I turn the switch on, and immediately there is light. There is a power in the wire that is to me-ward, that is available to me.

The organ is quiet but there is a power in the line that is organ-ward and organist-ward, and when Mr. Penny turns the switch we have music for our closing hymn. We sing together by power generated at Niagara Falls. You cannot hear the thunder of Niagara, but you can hear the diapason of the organ, which is simply a transformation of the Niagara thunder.

If we come as poor sinners we can have all the power of Heaven for salvation, and best of all, you will not get any electric light bill at the end of the month. Salvation is without money and without price.

"Jesus paid it all,
   All to Him I owe;
Sin had left a crimson stain,
   He washed it white as snow.
For nothing good have I,
   Whereby Thy grace to claim;
I'll wash my garments white,
   In the blood of Calvary's Lamb."

May the Lord help you to yield yourselves to Him.

                     —T. T. Shields

4. Christ Is Available to the Poorest Sinner

Some years ago I was conducting meetings in Evansville, Indiana, with Dr. Earnest Reveal at the Evansville Rescue Mission. A few days before I arrived in the city, some of the men of the Mission had decided to put on the doors of his garage a special device to open the doors automatically.

Dr. Reveal was a crippled man. He wore steel braces on his limbs and walked with a crutch and a cane. It was very difficult for him to get out of his car and walk any distance. Therefore, they thought it would be a fine thing if they put automatic doors on the garage; doors that would open when the car approached them, and doors that could be closed by the simple pressing of a button.

When I arrived in Evansville, Dr. Reveal told me about his garage doors. I listened to his elaborate story and as he told it, I thought that the automatic doors were made for just one person, Dr. Reveal.

A few days after that I drove his car down the street, turned into the driveway toward his garage, and the doors opened for me. I thought that perhaps there was some special gadget on his car that caused his doors to open, so I tried my car and the doors opened the same way.

Christ is available to the poorest sinner, the most despised one, the most wretched soul in the world. He is available to the self-righteous, the dignified, the self-assured person as well. Simply come to Him, come in repentance and faith—come receiving Him. He will give you everlasting life.

                     —Lee Roberson

5. The Secret Was That He Knew the Shepherd

The story is told of an outstanding actor who was asked to entertain one evening at an immense dinner party. As the great actor arose to speak the room was filled with excitement as the eager guests anticipated his message.

The star of the day said that he was going to recite the Twenty-third Psalm. This he did in a dramatic and eloquent manner. As soon as he had finished the chamber roared with applause as the audience arose in a standing ovation.

The next speaker of the evening was an elderly white-haired man who was bowed and feeble, worn by many long years of steadfast, patient labor as a missionary. A hush fell over the audience as he arose. After a moment's silence he said humbly, "I, too, would like to recite the Shepherd's Psalm."

Then, lifting his face slightly toward Heaven he closed his eyes and began:

> "The Lord is my shepherd; I shall not want.
> He maketh me to lie down in green pastures: he leadeth me beside the still waters.
> He restoreth my soul: he leadeth me in the paths of righteousness for his name's sake.
> Yea, though I walk through the valley of the shadow of death,
> I will fear no evil: for thou art with me; thy rod and thy staff they comfort me.
> Thou preparest a table before me in the presence of mine enemies: thou anointest my head with oil; my cup runneth over.
> Surely goodness and mercy shall follow me all the days of my life: and I will dwell in the house of the Lord for ever."

When the servant of the Lord finished, a pin could have been heard if one had dropped on the floor. This time there was no applause. There was standing ovation. Not a sound was heard. Yet, throughout the room there was not a dry eye. Tears were flowing freely.

Shortly afterward, a man approached the outstanding actor and said, "I don't understand. You both said the same thing. Your presentation was perfect in every way. Yet, when he spoke in his halting, imperfect manner, people were moved too deeply for words. What made the difference?"

The actor hesitated and then replied, "The answer is simple. I knew the Twenty-third Psalm and I knew it well, but he knows the Shepherd!"

Do you know the shepherd? If not, will you receive the Lord Jesus Christ today as your personal Saviour?

The Lord Jesus said:

"I am the door: by me if any man enter in, he shall be saved, and shall go in and out, and find pasture" (John 10:9).

—Billy Apostolon

6. It Was Thought They Could
Be Saved at Another Time

The steamship *Central American,* on a voyage from New York to San Francisco, sprang a lead in mid-ocean. A vessel, seeing her signal of distress, bore down towards her. Perceiving her danger to be imminent, the captain of the rescue ship spoke to the *Central American,* asking, "What is amiss?"

"We are in bad repair, and going down; lie by till morning," was the answer.

"Let me take your passengers on board now," said the would be rescuer.

As it was night, the captain of the Central American did not like to transfer his passengers, lest some might be lost in the confusion, and, thinking that they could keep afloat some hours longer, replied, "Lie by till morning."

Once again the captain of the rescue ship called, "You had better let me take them now."

"Lie by till morning" was sounded back through the trumpet. About an hour and a half later her lights were missed, and, though no sound was heard, the *Central American* had gone down, and all on board perished because it was thought they could be saved at another time.

While salvation is offered afresh to you now, dear friend, let me bid you speedily to obey the promptings of God's Spirit, and:

Hasten, hasten to be blest,
    Stay not for the morrow's sun;

Lest perdition thee arrest,
Ere the morrow is begun.

—Leslie Greening
Evangelist of Dorset, England

7. Mighty Sinners Saved by Mighty Grace

I remember reading once of a person who dreamed a
dream when in great distress of mind about religion. He
thought he stood in the outer court of Heaven, and he saw a
glorious host marching up the steps of light, singing hymns
and bearing the banners of victory. They passed by him, and
entered through the gates, and he heard, in the distance,
sweet strains of music.

"Who are they?" he asked. "Don't you know?" was the
reply. "They are the goodly fellowship of the Prophets, who
have gone to be with God." He heaved a deep sigh, as he said,
"Alas! I am not one of them, and shall never be, and cannot
enter there."

By and by there came another band, equally lovely in
appearance and equally triumphant, robed in white. "Who
are these?" he cried with wistful expectancy. "They are the
goodly fellowship of the Apostles." "Alas," he said, as they
passed within the portal, "I belong not to that fellowship,
and I cannot enter there."

He still waited and lingered, in the hope that he might yet
go in; but the next multitude did not encourage him, for they
were the noble army of Martyrs. He could not go with them,
nor wave their palm branches.

He waited still, and saw that the next was a company of
preachers of the gospel and earnest Christian workers, but he
felt he could not go in with them.

Hope of entrance seemed to have gone, when at last, as he
walked, he saw a larger host than all the rest put together

marching and singing melodiously, and in front walked the woman that was a sinner, and the thief that died upon the cross. He looked long, and saw there Manasseh, and the like; and when they entered he could see who they were, and he thought, "There will be shouting about them." But to his astonishment it seemed as if all Heaven was rent with seven-fold shouts as they passed in. The angels said to him, These are they that were *mighty sinners, saved by mighty grace."* Then he said, "Blessed be God! I can go in with them." So he awoke.

Will you enter the heavenly protals as "a sinner saved by grace?" Grace is unmerited favor. Accept Christ, yield to Him, give Him the government of your life, and you will stand and bask in the full radiance of the grace of the King of Heaven eternally.

—Charles Haddon Spurgeon

8. The Man Who Laughed When He Was Warned

A man ventured to walk out amid high rocks that jutted out into the sea. He was not aware of any danger, but another man was and called, "Hello there! The tide is rising and you have passed the last place through which you can escape. You had better turn back now."

The man laughed at the warning and walked on. After a while he thought it was time to turn back, but when he neared the place where he had been warned, his escape was cut off. He tried to climb up upon rocks but they were too high and wet. He was trapped. The tide of water kept rising until it reached his chin, and finally, with a wild shriek for help, he perished.

"Fool he was," you say. Yes, but friend, the tides of eternity are rising. Those only will be saved who get on the Rock of Ages, the Lord Jesus Christ, before it is too late. Now is the time to turn to God. Don't venture another hour. Heed God's tender and urgent appeal and warning:

"Say unto them, As I live, saith the Lord God, I have no pleasure in the death of the wicked; but that the wicked turn from his way and live: turn ye, turn ye from your evil ways; for why will ye die?" (Ezek. 33:11).

If you do not respond, what sensible and reasonable answer can you give? The answer is "None." Won't you say, "Realizing that I am a sinner, lost and far from God, I believe that Jesus Christ died for sinners, hence he died for me and rose from the dead to be my Saviour and Lord. Therefore, I, here and now, receive Him into my heart by faith to be my Saviour and risen Lord. By sincerely so doing, I believe He has saved me and I am now a child of God."

—The Radio Family Chat

9. How Christ Changes a Man

Years ago, some of my young people were holding an open air meeting at the Raven Hill Memorial Park in Belfast, Northern Ireland. It is convenient to where I preach. I was standing listening to these young men and women testify, and I saw a poor man come up the road, under the influence of liquor, and he was holding onto the railings, pulling himself along. I went over and laid my hand upon his shoulder. I said, "Friend, I'd like to tell you that Jesus Christ really loves you."

He looked at me, and with a thick tongue said, "You don't know me. If you knew who I was, you wouldn't even speak to me."

I said, "Yes, I would. I want to tell you of One who knows everything about you but loves you with an everlasting love, and His name is the Lord Jesus Christ. Let's go down to church, and we'll have prayer, and I'll tell you more about Jesus."

He said, "I'm not fit to go into any church building."

I said, "You are absolutely fit, for you know that you are a sinner."

He said, "I couldn't walk."

I said, "I could carry you." So I carried him. People think

I'm a fool anyway, so I might as well live up to my reputation! I carried him down the road.

I believe in this gospel I'm preaching. It's a transforming gospel. I often talk to Brother Joe. He's a member of our committee now, an honored man of God. He is well known on the Raven Hill Road. Everybody knows Joe Black. I said, "Joe, what happened when you got in the church?"

"Well, you put me into a room and you left me. You went into the outer building and started praying. When I heard you praying, I started to be sober, and then I started to think, and then, I got on my knees and I started to pray, too."

God really saved him. Let me emphasize that to you, and if you haven't got Jesus Christ, you haven't got life. You can have everything and anything, but you haven't got life. My earnest prayer is that you will receive Him, that you will be saved from the wrath to come, delivered from your sins, and that you will be born again eternally, of the Holy Ghost. May God do that mighty work in the hearts of sinners for Jesus' sake!

—Ian Paisley, Presbyterian Pastor of Belfast, Ireland.

10. A Wonderful Picture of What Jesus Has Done

I had the privilege of hearing Harry Ironside, former pastor of the Moody Church, preach many times before he died. There has never been a greater Bible teacher than Dr. Ironside. He lost his eyesight before he died. He made a trip to Australia and died on that trip, many miles from home. He used to tell this true story.

He said, "One time he saw something in the State of Texas that he just could not figure out. He was visiting a sheep ranch and saw something that looked like a deformity to him. It looked like a little lamb with four front feet, four back feet, and two heads. He stood there marvelling at it. He said to the rancher, 'Now there is a deformity if I ever saw one. I sure can't figure that out. What kind of a monstrosity is that?'

"The rancher laughed and said, 'That isn't a deformity at all. Actually, preacher, that is one of the most wonderful things that ever happened on this ranch. Let me tell you about it.

"There was a ewe lamb that had a little baby and her baby died. There was another ewe lamb that had a little baby and she died. We thought the thing to do was to give the lamb with no mother to the mother who had no baby. We put the little lamb with no mother in with the ewe that lost her baby and she wouldn't have a thing to do with it. She ducked her head, pushed it away and wanted no part of it. One of my men went out to where the little lamb was that had died, and skinned it as best as he could. He brought it back and tied it around the little baby lamb. We put it back with the mother whose baby died. She thinks that little lamb is hers. She loves it, nurses it and is taking care of it.'

"Dr. Ironside said, 'I never saw a more wonderful picture of what Jesus had done for me.' "

You take any man or woman and put them in the holy presence of an infinite God, clothed in their own righteousness and no matter how good they are, God Almighty will say, "Out of my presence." But, thank God, the Bible says that Jesus, to the believer, has been made our righteousness. If you are saved, you are clothed in the spotless righteousness of Jesus Christ and you are just as clean in the sight of God as if you had never committed a sin. When God looks from Heaven, He sees me clothed in the righteousness of the Son of God.

—Tom Malone,
President-Founder of Midwestern Baptist Seminary,
and pastor of Emmanuel Baptist Church, Pontiac, Michigan.

11. How a Young Methodist Evangelist Was Saved

In a Texas town I sat one night in the home of a most brilliant intellect, a marvelous personality—a young Methodist evangelist.

Twelve o'clock came. Then one. Then two. Three! Then four, and daybreak, and at seven his wife came in and announced breakfast.

I said, "I must go and get a little sleep. I speak at ten. Then this afternoon and again tonight." I asked him to go to my room. I gave him T. T. Martin's, *God's Plan with Men.* He was at the afternoon Bible lecture. He had finished the book. He asked me, after the lecture, to go for a walk with him. We walked three miles up the railroad. We walked back. In the lower edge of the railroad we sat down on a pile of cross ties.

He said, "I see salvation is only and alone in the fact Christ died for my sins. I would give a million worlds to rejoice in it like you do."

I said, "Why can't you?"

He said, "How can I when I live in the mortal fear of losing it?"

I said, "Can't the same Christ who died for you, to save you, and rose again—can't he keep you?"

He said, "But, if man in the garden was perfect, and he sinned and fell, and in redemption we are put back on a par with man in the garden, why can't we sin and fall?"

I said, "We· not only can, but we will. Every time man is put back on a par with man in the garden, he will sin and fall."

"But," I said, "the angels are God's creatures, but not God's children."

> "For unto which of the angels said he at any time, Thou art my Son, this day have I begotten thee? And again, I will be to him a Father, and he shall be to me a Son?" (Heb. 1:5).

Yet man in the garden was a lower creature of God than angels.

> "For thou hast made him a little lower than the angels, and hast crowned him with glory and honor" (Ps. 8:5)

Man, the lower of the two, sinned and fell. Myriads of angels sinned and fell also. There is no redemption for fallen angels.

> "For if God spared not the angels that sinned, but cast them down to hell, and delivered them into chains of darkness, to be reserved unto judgment" (II Peter 2:4). "But when the fulness of the time was come, God sent forth his Son, made of a woman, made under the law" (Gal. 4:4).

There was a deathly pause. That young preacher evangelist

ripped out a yell to the top of his voice—"Glory," and his head fell over on my shoulder as he sobbed and cried and cried and sobbed for joy.

—A. D. Muse

12. She Had Religion but She Was Lost

She was a lovely young woman in her early twenties, graduate of a university, and a school teacher. She was a vigorous, intensely alert, and capable person. A Christian worker talked to her about her soul.

Confidently she smiled at the Christian worker. "I have always been religious," she said. "My people were religious before me. Among my earliest memories are those connected with church and Sunday School. In fact, I received a prize one time for having had a perfect attendance record in church and Sunday School for five straight years. Then, in my late teens I began to teach classes of smaller girls. Yes, sir, I have a good religious background."

Something about this courteous young woman's statement made the Christian worker uneasy. There was something lacking, something about it that did not measure up. Gently, the Christian worker brought up the subject of personal salvation, the new birth, and regeneration. And the Christian worker talked of the atonement, the sin-offering of Jesus on the cruel cross, and of the empty tomb of the Son of God. Then said that something had to happen in the heart in order for one to be saved from his sins.

The eyes of this young woman opened wide and an expression of puzzlement came to her face. The Christian worker was talking of things foreign to her. She had almost no knowledge of the greater realities of the Spirit. A few minutes of kind probing told him that this lovely, intelligent, religious girl knew almost as little about salvation as some savage in a distant jungle.

Yet, she had spent almost all of her childhood in one church and under the ministry of one pastor. What on earth had that pastor talked about for all those years. Hundreds of times this young woman had sat under his preaching and in his Sunday School, yet she might as well have been in Africa as far as spiritual knowledge was concerned. She had religion but she was lost.

Is this true of you? Do you have religion, but are lost? If so, then by personal faith receive the Lord Jesus Christ as your Saviour.

—The Pastor's Friend

13. The Wages of Sin Is Death

John and Mack were "on vacation," as they said, for the summer. They were friendly young men and very diligent in picking up "odd jobs" to help the storekeepers in the little town in which they had chosen to spend their free time.

One merchant in particular favored these "vacationers" with many such "odd jobs" and as the summer wore on, they spent much time in his store. The two young men exerted themselves to be pleasant and helpful and they soon won the confidence of their benefactor. Indeed, so much did the merchant trust them that before the end of summer he became quite confidential with them.

One night as the storekeeper was preparing to close up, he explained to his young helpers that he never left money in the safe as it could be blown open. Instead, as he showed them, he removed some boxes from an upper shelf, and placed his day's receipts carefully in a smaller box among the merchandise. Just as carefully he replaced the merchandise and boxes, commenting smugly that "no one would think to look there." However, one important thing he failed to mention. Just two blocks away was the police station, and connected by direct line with it was every door and window of this store. Any tampering with these openings would immediately set off an alarm at the police station.

When Saturday night approached, the young men watched the storekeeper as he, more carefully than usual, hid the bag containing his day's receipts among the merchandise. Surely Satan, the enemy of souls was at hand to tempt the two with the prospect of "easy money," and, having no scruples nor conscience in the matter they were taken captive of him at his will.

In the dark of that midnight these trusted friends, as the deceived merchant had called them, quietly forced open the door and as quickly as possible seized the heavy bag of money. However, to their amazement the midnight air was suddenly full of screeching sirens; and as they frantically sought to escape, they found police cars and officers blocking every exit.

Grabbing the money bag, one of the thieves raced out the back door. There a policeman spied him and gave chase. Calling to the running man, the officer ordered, "Halt!" Four times he uttered the usual command, but to no avail. The thief ran faster, trying to dodge the officer's bullets as they whined at hand. Four times the officer called, and four times the shots rang out. One hit the target, and the dead thief was found lying face down, still gripping the money bag from which the stolen money was spilling. His partner was found, too, crouching among the merchandise that had proved to be such a poor hiding place.

In both cases, sin had claimed its wages. For one young man, a blighted life and years of imprisonment. For the slain thief, the awful doom of death. How terrible for a lost sinner to fall into the hands of the living God!

> "And as it is appointed unto men once to die, but after this the judgment" (Heb. 9:27).

Sinner, God's love follows you as you race to your doom. Tenderly He calls and would bring you to Himself. Heed Him now before it is too late, for He says:

> "All that the Father giveth me shall come to me; and him that cometh to me I will in no wise cast out" (John 6:37).
>
> —Author Unknown

14. The Man Who Rejected Salvation at the Twelfth Hour

In one of D. L. Moody's meetings a man once raised his hand for prayer. The evangelist went to him and said, "I am glad you have decided to be a Christian."

"No," said the man, "I have not, but you pray for me, and I will later on."

His address was taken, and later when the man was ill Mr. Moody visited him. During this visit Mr. Moody again encouraged him to make a decision for Christ.

"No," said the man, "I will not decide now. People will only say I was frightened into receiving Christ while I'm sick."

The man recovered but before long he suffered a severe relapse. Mr. Moody visited him again and put his need of Christ before him.

"It is too late," he said.

"But," Mr. Moody replied, "there is mercy at the eleventh hour."

"Mr. Moody," the sick man answered, "this is not the eleventh hour. It is the twelfth." A few hours later the man was dead.

Mr. Moody said, "We fear we wrapped him in a Christless shroud, put him in a Christless coffin, buried him in a Christless grave, and if this be so, he went to a Christless eternity."

> "He that being often reproved hardeneth his neck, shall suddenly be destroyed, and that without remedy" (Prov. 29:1).

—Billy Apostolon
(selected and adapted)

15. He Took Advantage of the Opportunity

I knew a young freckle-faced boy in Missouri once who was working in a roundhouse. He didn't go around the saloons at night. He studied telegraphy. He studied about the engines, he was always studying. He was always minding his own business.

There are two reasons why folks don't mind their own business. One is that they haven't any business. The other is that they haven't any mind.

An engineer on the railroad had his little child in the cab

22

of the engine and he stepped off to do something, and the little boy did what he had seen his father do. He threw the lever over and opened the throttle wide and the engine jumped forward and down the track it went, a wild engine.

Jim happened to be in the telegraph office with a friend studying telegraphy. The operator was out, but Jim heard the message going over the wire that the wild engine was coming. He ran out and jumped on a switch engine and started out to meet the other engine.

Everyone said that he would be killed. Why didn't he stay here? As the other engine approached, he reversed his engine and started to back away from it. Gradually he got his engine to run the same speed as the wild engine. When the engines came together he reversed his engine so that it was pressing hard against the other one, crept back in his cab, then over it to the other engine. When they got there the little boy was sitting on Jim's knee laughing. Jim was made an engineer on the spot. Was it an accident that Jim did that? No, he seized an opportunity that he had been preparing for.

Some day it will be too late for you to be saved. The opportunity will be gone forever. The water that runs past the mill will never return to go past it again. Become a Christian. Live for others and think of the good you can do.

—E. J. Bulgin

16. Sir James Y. Simpson's Personal Testimony

When I was a boy at school I saw a sight I can never forget—a man tied to a cart and dragged before the people's eyes through the streets of my native town, his back torn and bleeding from the lash. It was a shameful punishment. For many offenses? No! For one offense. Did any of the towns-men offer to divide the lashes with him? No! He who committed the offense bore the penalty of all. It was the penalty of a changing human law, for it was the last instance of its infliction.

When I was a student at the university I saw another sight I can never forget—a man brought out to die. His arms were pinioned, his face was already pale as death—thousands of eager eyes were on him as he came up from the jail in sight. Did any man ask to die in his room (stead)? Did any friend come and loose the rope, and say, "Put it around my neck, I will die instead?" No! He underwent the sentence of the law. For many offenses? No! For one offense. He had stolen a money parcel from a stagecoach. He broke the law at one point, and died for it. It was the penalty of a changing human law. In this case also it was the last instance of capital punishment being inflicted for that offense.

I saw another sight I shall never forget—myself a sinner, standing on the brink of ruin, condemned to eternal punishment in the lake of fire. For one sin? No! For many, many sins committed against the unchanging laws of God. I looked again, and behold, Jesus Christ became my Substitute. He bore in His own body on the tree all the punishment for my sin. He died on the cross that I might live in glory. He suffered, the Just for the unjust, that He might bring me to God. He redeemed me from the curse of the law. I sinned and was condemned to eternal punishment. He bore the punishment and I am free.

The law of God required a perfect righteousness which I never had. Again, I looked unto Him and found that Christ is the end of the law for righteousness to every one that believeth. The law required spotless purity and I was defiled with sin. Again, I looked unto Him who loved us and washed us from our sins in His own blood. I was a child of disobedience, a child of wrath.

"But as many as received him, to them gave he power to become the sons of God, even to them that believe on his name:" (John 1:12).

I found in Him not only my Substitute, but the full supply of every need of my life. I long to tell you of this Saviour.

"Neither is there salvation in any other: for there is none other name under heaven given among men, whereby we must be saved" (Acts 4:12).

—Sir James Y. Simpson, M.D.
The Discoverer of Chloroform

17. The Verse That Has Brought

Peace to Thousands

At the close of a gospel address a Christian worker spoke to a young man who, he thought, seemed to be impressed by the message. The Christian soon found that he had not heard a word, for he was deaf and dumb. However, the Lord's servant was not hindered by that difficulty, knowing a little of the sign language, he just gave him the simple message, "God loves you."

The young man looked at God's servant with a vacant stare, and shaking his head, he replied by signs, "No, no, I don't believe it. I know God hates me."

"However, can you say so?" the Christian worker asked.

"I went to a church, and the preacher gave an address. It was interpreted to us. He told us that 'God would forever cast us into Hell if we did not live holy lives, and keep His holy commandments.' Ever since I heard that, I have not opened a Bible, I was afraid and, of course, I never went to that church again."

"What did you come here for? You could not hear anything."

"I don't know why I came."

"Shall I tell you?" the Christian worker asked.

"If you know, you can."

"Well, dear fellow, you were drawn by an unseen Person that you might know that 'God loves you.' "

"I wish that I did know it."

Taking up a Bible, the Christian worker turned to John 3:16, that grand old verse, which has brought peace to thousands:

> "For God so loved the world, that he gave his only begotten Son, that whosoever believeth in him should not perish, but have everlasting life."

The light seemed to shine in little by little, but still there was darkness. Turning to many other Scriptures which spoke of God's love, the Christian worker pointed him to I John 4:17, 19:

> "Herein is our love made perfect, that we may have boldness in the day of judgment: because as he is, so are we in this world."

> "We loved him, because he first loved us."

Again and again the young man read them, and the change in his countenance was wonderful. Taking his notebook out, he wrote down all the passages that the Christian worker had pointed him to. When saying "good-by" he added, "I see it all now and, although dumb, I can praise God in my heart for the gift of Jesus."

Are you deaf, spiritually deaf? Or are your ears open to hear the voice of the Son of God? God loves you, and has shown that love in giving His Son to die for you. He delights not in the death of a sinner. If He did, there would have been no need for the Lord Jesus to die. Make no mistake about it. God loves you. Own yourself as a lost sinner, and let that love draw you to His heart.

> "All that the Father giveth me shall come to me; and him that cometh to me I will in no wise cast out" (John 6:37).

—Selected

18. Sincerity Is Not Enough

The pilot of a private plane, R. C. Corder, radioed for "Approach landing" instructions to the airport in Ontario, California. The Federal Aviation Agency Controller instructed Corder to drop from a safe altitude of 10,000 feet to 7,200 feet. Corder dropped altitude and crashed into a mountain near San Bernadino, California. Both he and his two passengers were killed.

"A one-in-a-million case of mistaken identity," FAA officials explained. "The controller mistook on his radar screen another plane to be Corder's." The reason was that Corder had failed to make a position report to another air controller along his route.

Here was a case where no one could be charged with insincerity. The airport controller sincerely thought he was tuned to the wave length of the plane on his radar screen, when actually he was tuned to the R. C. Corder plane.

The pilot of the plane on the radar screen was innocently unaware of his part in the impending tragedy. Corder sincerely thought he had received the right instructions. His passengers were just as sincere. However, three men were killed because of a "sincere error."

Sincerity is not enough.

> "There is a way which seemeth right unto a man, but the end thereof are the ways of death" (Prov. 14:12).
>
> —James C. Hefley
> in the *Gospel Herald*

19. The Man Who Was

Sylvester Horn's Last Convert

The following touching story concerning the death of Rev. Sylvester Horne, was told by one of the British delegates to the Pilgrim Tercentenary in Boston.

This delegate was traveling on a St. Lawrence steamer on his way to the Council. Suddenly he remembered the tragic circumstances connected with the death years ago of Mr. Horne.

Addressing the captain one day he asked, "Do you happen to remember, Captain, the death a few years ago on one of these St. Lawrence river boats of an English preacher named Sylvester Horne?"

The captain answered quietly but with deep feeling, "I certainly do. It was on this very boat." He then showed the English visitor the precise spot where the saintly man fell. "I chanced to see him fall and ran toward him. He died instantly. His wife holding his head called out in agony, 'Are you dead?' Then turned to me, 'Captain, is my husband really dead?' I nodded, yes, and ordered some sailors to carry the body into my cabin. Come on in, I want you to see the cabin."

As the minister entered the captain's room he noticed a beautifully framed photograph of the deceased prophet. Then he resumed the story: "But when we brought his body into this cabin, that was not the end of the tale. Mrs. Horne came in and immediately kneeled down beside his body.

"She turned to me, 'Captain, you must kneel.'

"I was not a kneeling man, in fact, I was altogether indifferent to religion, but I hesitated only a second, then knelt. Her prayer was the simplest, most beautiful, most natural prayer I ever heard. She mentioned all the children by name, the church and various causes that had been dear to her husband's heart. Do you know, I have never been able to escape from that prayer. It brought me to Christ. I am now a professing Christian, and whenever I can I attend the little church of which I have become a member. I was Sylvester Horne's last convert."

—Selected

20. God's Offer Is for Today

An earnest Christian doctor one day called to see an old man that he had frequently visited before.

Old John was suffering from an attack of bronchitis. Dr. S------- made the necessary inquiries, and, after promising to get some medicine ready when called for, he was about to say "good-by" when John's wife inquired: "When must John take the medicine, sir?"

"Let me see. You are not very ill. Suppose you begin to take it this day a month."

"This day a month, sir?" cried both in astonishment.

"Yes, why not? Is that too soon?"

"Too soon! Why, sir, I may be dead then!" said John.

"That is true, but you must remember you really are not very bad yet. Still, perhaps you had better begin to take it in a week."

"But, sir," cried John in great perplexity, "begging your pardon, sir, I might not live a week."

"Of course, you may not, John, but very likely you will, and the medicine will be in the house. It will keep, and if you find yourself getting worse, you could take some. I won't charge anything for it. If you should feel worse tomorrow evening, you might begin then."

"Sir, I may be dead tomorrow!"

"When would you propose to begin then, John?"

"Well, sir, I thought you would tell me to begin today."

"Begin today by all means," said Dr. S-------, kindly. "I only wanted to show you how false your own reasoning is, when you put off taking the medicine which the Great Physician has provided for your sin-sick soul. Just think how long you have neglected the remedy He has provided. For years you have turned away from the Lord Jesus. You have said to yourself, 'next week' or 'next year' or 'when I am on my deathbed, I will seek the Lord'; anytime rather than the present. Yet the present is the only time that you are sure of. God's offer is only for 'today.'"

> "... behold, now is the accepted time; behold, now is the day of salvation" (II Cor. 6:2).

You may be dead tomorrow.

—Herald of Salvation

21. How William Jennings Bryan

Saved a Young Man from Suicide

Have you heard how William Jennings Bryan, who three times was a contender for the office of President of the United States, saved a young man from suicide? Listen to the young man as he tells the story in his own words.

"I had been engaged by a large firm in the Orient at a salary that was a small fortune to me, and as I bade my weeping mother and sweetheart, goodbye, I said cheerfully, 'You know it will only be for one year and we will then have a small fortune to begin our life together.'

"The year was up and to induce me to stay with them, the firm offered to almost double my salary but I said, 'I have given my promise to my loved ones that I would return in one year and I must keep my word.

"Happily I started for home but as I stepped on deck of the little special steamer at Honolulu en route, there was handed to me a letter that had been waiting for me for some days. It read, 'Knowing you were on your way to the States, we did not know how to reach you but knew that you would be stopping at Honolulu. We are pained to inform you that your mother and the one who was to be your wife have both suddenly succumbed to the epidemic of influenza and passed away. The funeral service was conducted by your mother's pastor.'

"It seemed to take the heart out of me. Mother and sweetheart gone, of what value was my little fortune now?

"The same day an announcement was read by the captain which had been signed by the governor that William Jennings Bryan, worn out with a long lecturing tour was to come on board for rest and recreation and to give him the most cordial welcome.

"I knew the man, had attended his lectures in the past and greatly appreciated them but, now I had no interest in anyone or anything. The constant recurring thought of a grave beneath the blue waters of the Pacific followed me. What was there to live for now?

"I paced the deck listlessly but could not refrain from watching this truly great but humble man. I knew he was a man of prayer and would spend much time in his stateroom with closed door and I wondered.

"Late one night when all was quiet I stood by the ship's railing with my mind made up to take the fatal plunge, when I heard soft footsteps and a hand was gently laid upon my shoulder and with pathos in his voice he said, 'Young man, I have been watching you for days. I knew what was in your mind. You have some deep heart sorrow and were about to take a fatal plunge and end it all, as you thought, but there is a better way. Let me pray for you.' Half unconsciously I sank to my knees and shook from head to foot as that man prayed Heaven and earth together. I never heard such a prayer, the power of God fell till all thoughts of suicide left me and I saw I could go home right where mother and sweetheart had labored among the poor and use my little fortune just as they would have done in ministering to their needs, and life again seemed to look worthwhile.

"Thanks be unto God and to William Jennings Bryan who came to me that night and saved me from a suicide's grave."

As this young man was saved from physical death, the

Lord will save you from spiritual death. Listen to His precious Words:

> ". . . I am the resurrection, and the life: he that believeth in me, though he were dead, yet shall he live: And whosoever liveth and believeth in me shall never die. Believest thou this?" (John 11:25, 26).

Will you receive the Lord Jesus Christ now as your personal Saviour?

—Billy Apostolon

22. How God Brings Christ to Seeking Souls

Tomas Arriaga wasn't satisfied. Even though he had a wonderful wife, Juana, and six lovely children, and a reasonably good job, there was a strange feeling of emptiness in his heart.

One day while listening to Lester Hershey on the Spanish radio program, *Luz y Verdad,* he heard that a calendar with a picture of Christ on it could be had free by writing to the broadcast.

Soon the calendar found a place beside the virgins and saints that adorned the wall of the Arriaga cement-block cottage in rural Texas.

Not only had the calendar found its way into the home, but with it came an invitation to study a Spanish Bible course.

Tomas told his wife to enroll "out of politeness" since they thought it would not have been courteous to refuse after getting the calendar free.

After the first lessons arrived, not only did Juana study them but Tomas was soon studying, too. Before much time had passed Juana responded to the Holy Spirit's call and she became a Christian.

With this growing interest, Weldon Martin, who directs the radio branch office in Texas, was led to visit the Arriaga home.

As a result of the visit of Mr. and Mrs. Martin, Tomas

yielded his life to Christ. Then Tomas and Juana both wanted Christian fellowship, which they found at the small church of which Weldon Martin is pastor.

September 9, 1962, was an important date in the life of Tomas and Juana, for on that day they were baptized. Since then they are witnessing of Christ to others.

The first note from the Arriagas asking for a calendar seemed very insignificant. But as Pastor Weldon Martin says, "Theirs is a thrilling story of how God used radio, Bible correspondence courses, and the local church to bring Christ to seeking souls."

—Informer

23. Suppose That the Brakes Fail

A railway train was climbing a very steep grade up the mountainside and a lady passenger became very nervous. As the conductor passed through the car she clutched his sleeve and asked:

"Conductor, suppose anything goes wrong with the engine while we are climbing the mountain, what will happen to us?"

"The air brakes are good, madam."

"But suppose something goes wrong with them?"

"We have other brakes, madam, and they are in good condition."

"But suppose all the brakes fail, what then?"

"That, madam," answered the conductor earnestly, "depends upon how you have lived."

We smile at the woman's foolish fears. Yet, how many things depend upon how we have lived? You cannot enjoy the comfort and security of the child of God unless you let Jesus into your life. You can accept Christ as your Saviour and find "an anchor for the soul, both sure and steadfast."

People are often so wise for their bodies and yet so foolish for their souls. So busy with the rush for material things that they forget the spiritual and fail to remember that the future life is so largely dependent upon the present manner of living.

Listen!

"But as many as received him, to them gave he power to become the sons of God, even to them that believe on his name" (John 1:12)

Will you do this now?

—T. DeCourcy Rayner

24. Won to Christ by a Preacher in Tennis Shoes

I was out mowing the yard one day while pastoring in Texas. Our church was the largest in our city. One out of seven people in town belonged to our church, and I saw my members quite often.

When I mow the yard, I'm not quite a beauty queen! That day I had on a tee shirt with a hole in the shoulder and one right under the arm. I had on a pair of old tennis shoes with holes in them and a pair of trousers with patches in the knee, and I think I had on either a golf cap or a fishing hat. I was a tragic looking thing, a sight to behold!

My wife came out in the yard and said, "Honey, would you go get some sugar from the neighbor down the street?"

I said, "All right, I'll do it." So I got the cup and marched down there with my tennis shoes, my fishing cap, and a hole in my tee shirt. We were very close friends to the folks, so we never knocked. I walked in and said, "Hey! Anybody home?"

There—thirteen people were at home—company all dressed up in suits and fine clothes. There I was! Imagine, a cup in my hand, a fishing hat on, a split tee shirt, a patch in my breeches, and a pair of tennis shoes on my feet!

I said, "Hello."

The lady looked at me. She looked at her company, and then announced, "This is my pastor."

I was horrified! I was humiliated! I wanted to evaporate, but I couldn't. Finally, I said, "Excuse me. I'm sorry." Then I got to thinking. Shoot! Just take over the conversation. Just act like you have good sense. So in I walked. "How do you do! How are you? Are you a Christian?" I went around the room asking the same question. Then, they got embarrassed.

I asked each person if he or she were a Christian. The last

one, a young man, said, "No, I'm not, but I've been thinking about it."

"Well," I said, "I can help you think about it right here." We knelt in the home and opened the Bible. He was converted. The next day he walked the aisle in our church, and he was baptized in the evening service.

> "That if thou shalt confess with thy mouth the Lord Jesus, and shalt believe in thine heart that God hat raised him from the dead, thou shalt be saved" (Rom 10:9).

> —Jack Hyles
> pastor of the First Baptist Church, Hammond, Indiana

25. A Greater Than Governor Nash

Offers a Pardon

A story is told of Governor Nash of the State of Ohio in years gone by. A young man had murdered his sweetheart because she would not marry him. After much pleading by the young man's mother, the governor promised her that he would call on her son who had been sentenced to death. Finally the governor stood before the convicted man, dressed in a Prince Albert coat causing the man to think that he was a preacher.

The governor, calling him by name, said, "I have come to talk with you." The prisoner replied, "I do not feel like talking," and then turned his back.

The governor replied, "I am sure you would talk if you knew who I am and why I have come."

The young man said, "Please go out, for I do not feel like talking."

The governor turned and went out. The warden entered and said, "How did you make out with the governor?"

He said, "Governor—what governor?"

"Why Governor Nash, that was the governor, himself."

"Oh," said the man, "if I had only known with whom I was talking!"

A greater than Governor Nash is here talking to you. He

wants to give you life—eternal life. The Bible says in Hebrews 12:25:

> "See that ye refuse not him that speaketh. For if they escaped not who refused him that spake on earth, so much more shall not we escape, if we turn away from him that speaketh from heaven."

Governor Nash was the only person who had power to pardon the condemned prisoner. What a pity that he rejected him!

Jesus is the only one to pardon sinners. Peter tells us in Acts 4:12:

> "Neither is there salvation in any other: for there is none other name under heaven given among men, whereby we must be saved."
>
> —Author Unknown

26. Sin Makes People Fear to Face God

It is said that a Hungarian king, finding himself on a certain day depressed and unhappy sent for his brother, a good-natured but rather indifferent prince. To him the king said, "I am a great sinner and fear to meet God." Here was a king facing Job's question, "What shall I do when God riseth up? And when he visiteth, what shall I answer Him?" (Job 31:14).

The prince only laughed at him and treated the matter as a joke, just the way people are doing now. This did not serve to relieve the royal unhappiness. When you get a vision of your guilt before God, you want help and your friends may laugh at your seriousness, but that will never answer the question. It was a custom in Hungary at that time that if the executioner at any hour sounded a trumpet before a man's door, it was a signal that he was to be led forth to be executed.

The king sent the executioner in the dead of the night to sound the fateful flast before his brother's door. The prince, awaking from sleep, realized its awful import. Quickly dressing, he stepped to the door and was seized by the executioner, and dragged pale and trembling into the king's presence. In an agony of terror he fell upon his knees before his brother and begged in what way he had offended him.

"My brother," answered the king, "if the sight of a human executioner is so terrible to you, shall not I, having grievously offended God, fear to be brought before the judgment of Christ."

The sense of sin makes us all fear to face God. We are reminded in the Bible that "It is a fearful thing to fall into the hands of the living God" (Heb. 10:31).

—O. A. Newlin

27. The Family That Was Won by a Smile

When I asked Mr. Moody what he thought of Spurgeon, he said:

"He is a perpetual stream of Christian sunlight. One Sunday morning in London," continued Mr. Moody, "Spurgeon said to me, just before he commenced his sermon, 'Moody, I want you to notice that family there in one of the front seats, and when we go home I want to tell you their story.'

"When we got home," said Moody, "I asked him for the story, and he said:

" 'All that family were won by a smile.'

" 'Well,' said he, 'as I was walking down a street one day, I saw a child at a window, it smiled, and I smiled, and we bowed. It was the same the second time; I bowed, she bowed. It was not long before there was another child, and I had got in a habit of looking and bowing, and pretty soon the group grew, and at last, as I went by, a lady was with them. I didn't know what to do. I didn't want to bow to her, but I knew the children expected it, and so I bowed to them all.

" 'The mother saw I was a minister, because I carried a Bible every Sunday morning. So the children followed me the next Sunday and found I was a minister. They thought I was the greatest preacher, and their parents must hear me.

" 'A minister who is kind to a child and gives him a pat on the head, why, the children will think he is the greatest preacher in the world. Kindness goes a great way. Finally, the father and mother and five children were converted, and they are going to join our church next Sunday.'

"Won to Christ by a smile!" said Moody. "We must get the wrinkles out of our brows, and we must have smiling faces, if we want to succeed in our work of love."

—Author Unknown

28. The Man Who Died without Hope

Lee R. Scarborough, late president of the Southwestern Baptist Theological Seminary tells the following which illustrates the truth that there are many who die without hope.

Dr. Scarborough said:

"In my pastorate at Abilene years ago in a great revival which I was holding in my church, I went as my custom was to see the people. I went into a hotel which was under new management. I went into the office and invited the proprietor who had just come to the town to make our church his church home.

"He was a big, fine looking man. He looked me in the face and said, 'Are you the pastor of that church?'

"I said, 'I am' and for two or three minutes I stood and heard him swear and curse preachers and churches and Christians.

"Then he walked back into the private room of his hotel. During that meeting God led back from twenty-seven years of backsliding his wife, led there by this wicked man. I led to Christ his son, who now, thank God, is preaching the gospel. I led to Christ his daughter who is a student in our Training School at Fort Worth.

"When that meeting was over, one day my telephone rang. That wife at the other end of the line said, 'Come.' I went to that hotel. I went into that family room. There stood the weeping wife and the sorrowing children. There lay that big strong man on his bed breathing his last. He had been suddenly taken with an incurable disease.

"His lips moved and his wife said, 'Put your ear to his lips and hear what he says.' I am sorry I did. A thousand times his dying words have run in my soul: 'Dying without hope. Dying without God. Dying without Christ—hopeless, hopeless!' For twenty-five times, I guess, his strength enabled him to say it, and then he went out into eternity."

Isn't this a sad incident. To die without hope. To die without God. To die without Christ as your personal Saviour. While you are living and God is speaking to you, will you accept Christ as your personal Saviour.

Remember the words of warning of our Lord Jesus Christ, how that he said:

> "I tell you, Nay: but, except ye repent, ye shall all likewise perish" (Luke 13:3, 5).

—Billy Apostolon

29. Today Is the Day of Salvation

"Will you decide now to accept Jesus Christ as your Lord and Saviour?" an earnest Christian asked a friend.

He seemed to have no answer. His head was bowed in thought. The pause became embarrassing.

"When will you decide?" was the next interrogation. "Twenty years from now?"

"No," came the answer, "It's not likely I'll live twenty years."

"Will you make it ten years from now?"

"No," said he, "I wouldn't dare say I'd have ten years to live."

"Well, suppose we set the time for five years from now! That will give you five years for self; the world, and Satan."

He was becoming more serious. "I know I should have been serving the Lord for many years," he said. "I don't want to say I'll delay for five years more."

"Then will you decide for Christ this time next year?"

"One never knows what may happen in a year, does he?" came the answer.

"Well, you might get by another month without the Lord! Of course, you'd lose the reward of service you might render Christ in that time, but—"

"I know I shouldn't wait a month—but not just now!" he said.

"How about this time tomorrow?"

The Christian's friend could not help but see how foolish he was making himself. Tears broke through and with a sob he said, "I will take Him now as my Saviour!"

Oh, what peace flooded that man's soul as we knelt side by side for a word of prayer, and as I opened the New Testament to show him the simple way of salvation from John 1:12.

> "But as many as received him, to them gave he power to become the sons of God, even to them that believe on his name."
>
> —Your Answer

30. The Man Who Was Arrested against His Will

We have often heard of men, women or even children, who in God's ways, have been used for special blessings to others around them. Could you ever believe that a fly, that undesirable, pestering insect, could be an instrument in God's hand to bring a soul to Him? Yes, our God in His infinite wisdom can use the smallest and weakest to confound the strong and mighty.

When the well known gospel preacher, John Wesley, was holding meetings in the city of Dublin, Ireland, a man was drawn to come to hear that outstanding speaker. Being fond of music, he came with the idea that he could stop his ears to the preaching and open them for the singing of the hymns.

All went well and according to his plan until a fly flew near, persistently settling itself on his face. This annoyed him so that he kept chasing it away with his hand. Believe it or not, that small lapse of time was put to a remarkable use, for the man's own good.

As he uncovered his ears to swat the fly, a solemn warning came from the preacher. Over and over the message sounded. God in His infinite mercy and love for lost souls, speaks once, yea, twice. Woe to those who close their ears and minds against Him. The warning was four times repeated:

> "He that hath ears to hear, let him hear" (Matt. 11:15).
> "Who hath ears to hear, let him hear" (Matt. 13:9).

"... Who hath ears to hear, let him hear" (Matt. 13:43).
"... He that hath ears to hear, let him hear" (Mark 4:9).

The man who was so determined not to hear was, in spite of himself, brought under the sound of God's voice. In spite of every hindrance, when God speaks, His words do not return unto Him void.

This man was arrested against his will. He was forced to take heed in such a way that he had no rest until he found peace with God through the Lord Jesus Christ.

"Incline your ear, and come unto me: hear, and your soul shall live . . ." (Isa. 55:3).

—Selected

31. How a Down and Out Sinner Was Saved

An old ragged unkempt tramp knocked at the back door of a New Hampshire home one morning, and asked for something to eat. The mother of the home invited the poor old fellow in to the kitchen to rest, and while preparing a good meal for him she learned that at one time he had a good home and a wife and children.

Drink had driven him from one sin to another until his family deserted him. He then drifted from place to place and deeper and deeper into sin until he had no desire or ambition to do anything but tramp and beg. He believed that no one cared what became of him and that it didn't matter much to himself either.

A small son in the home sat near the table watching the old man and finally walked over to the poor fellow and placed his little hand on the poor dirty, ragged coat sleeve and looked up at the sin marked face. *"Man, does you love Dod?"* he asked. He repeated the question several times and getting no reply said, *"Well, man Dod loves you."*

The tramp's eyes filled with tears and his hand trembled but he made no answer. The little boy then went to his room and returned with ten coppers that had been given to him for candy. He placed them in the hand of the old man saying;

"Man, this will buy some milk." The poor fellow's head went down and the tears of years were shed there.

He left the house without saying a word and was unheard of for many months. At last a letter in a cramped hand came addressed to the child saying, "Little one you saved me from Hell. After I left your house I walked along the country road and all I could hear was, *"Man, Dod loves you."* I fell asleep that night under a tree and dreamed of a fair curly haired child, with his little hand on my sleeve, saying over and over, *'Man Dod loves you.'"*

That was all I could hear and see for days, until I threw myself on the ground and wept all the hardness out of my heart. I saw again the man I used to be, the cozy home I had owned, the loving wife and the dear children that sin had taken from my side. I thought of all I had sacrificed to serve the devil and of what he had made me, who had once been pure and sweet as the little child who brought that message from God to me. I cried out, "Oh, God, if it isn't too late, make me a child once more and let me see that little lad in Heaven some day, if I never do down here."

"I have a job now and clothes and a place to sleep. I'm an old man and I won't be here long, but God bless you, child, because you led an old dirty tramp to God. I know when death comes and I reach the cold, dark river, a sweet childish voice will float out to me saying, *'Man, Dod loves you.'"*

What Christ did for that old dirty tramp, He can and will do for you, whether your sins be great or small.

> "Come now, and let us reason together, saith the Lord: though your sins be as scarlet, they shall be as white as snow; though they be red like crimson, they shall be as wool" (Isa. 1:18).

—Selected

32. Deliverance from Death Now or Never

There are districts in North England where the inhabitants live to a great extent upon the eggs of sea-birds, who build their nests among the high precipitous rocks on the sea coast and adjoining islands.

One of these hunters was, on one occasion, at his usual calling when he discovered a large nest some hundred feet below him upon a ledge of rock. The overhanging rock from which he could see the nest, made it very difficult to get at the spot, as, when letting himself down with a long rope, he would find it a difficult thing to get on to the rock, which was further inwards, or underneath, than the peak upon which he stood.

However, these professional hunters are so accustomed to difficulties of this sort, that he determined upon trying to reach the ledge. Accordingly, driving his large iron stake into the ground and fixing his rope 'round it he proceeded to let himself down over the cliff. Safely descending to the level of the nest, he was *suspended in midair by his rope.*

To reach the ledge it was necessary to commence swinging to and fro. This is only done by the action of the body; but by degrees a heavy enough swing to and fro was obtained to touch with his feet the ledge of rock. The next swing back he determined to try and land safely upon the ledge. As he approached, it was necessary to give a spring and balance himself so as to enable him to stand upright upon the ledge. This was just the difficulty; still, with skilled hands and steady brain, he safely accomplished it, but in congratulating himself he did not fully realize his position, and without thinking, *he let go of the rope by mistake.* The coil and seat attached to it swung back and with almost as great velocity as when he was in it.

In an instant he saw his position, and as quickly realized that *little short of death stared him in the face.* No one was above or near to let down another rope or to accomplish the same feat to reach the ledge as he had just done himself.

He saw the rope receding and then again approaching him with a return swing. In cases of great danger, thought is often as quick as lightning in realizing the necessity of action. He saw that if he did not give a spring off the ledge on to the rope on its first return, there might be no hope of catching it on the second return, certainly none on its third or following swings, as each time it would not come so near to him.

With one bound, just as the rope approached him, on its first return, he sprang from the ledge, and, nerved as it were from the very jaws of *death*, his presence of mind and muscle enabled him to hang on to it, and once again rest safely in the seat. He was rescued. Truly it had been *now or never!* Nothing could depict that scene or the impression that it left on the man's mind to see the rope swinging away and coming back, and, in an instant of time realizing not only his position but his *one chance.*

He might have missed it, and been dashed to pieces on the rocks some hundreds of feet below him.

It was the *supreme moment* of a lifetime, a definite crisis, and there are such moments—such spiritual crisis in the lives of many of us; a moment when the Holy Spirit draws very near and we have to use our will and decide whether we will give up sin and yield ourselves to Christ, or refuse His free gift of salvation and eternal life.

—Author Unknown

33. How a Texas Cowboy Got Saved

L. R. Scarborough was president of Southwestern Seminary in Fort Worth, Texas. He was a great preacher and soul winner. Years ago he was holding a revival meeting in the state of Texas. He had been out that day, mixing and mingling with the cowboys, trying to get acquainted with them and win them. That night one of them came. He had his cowboy boots and chaps on, his cowboy shirt and his hat in his hand. When he came into the meeting he sat down near the back.

Dr. Scarborough said that in his sermon that night, he preached for the soul of that man. He gave the invitation and the man made no response. He went back near the back and got the cowboy by the right arm and said to him, "Cowboy, I want you to be a Christian. I want you to be saved."

The cowboy jerked his right arm out of his hands, stalked out of the little church with his heavy heels on, and went on his way. The next norming, he got on his horse. He was riding along and his horse fell and pinned his right arm under the body of the horse and broke his arm.

That night he came back to the meeting. He came down the aisle with a broken arm, bandaged and in a sling. He said, "Preacher, last night I wrenched this broken arm from your grip, I turned my heart against Jesus Christ, and walked out of this building. I would like to give that right arm to you tonight, but I can't. So I'll give you my left arm. I want to be saved. God spoke to me under the body of that horse, with that right arm that I had wrenched from your hand. I said to God, 'If you will let me out of this, if you will save my life, if you will let me be rescued from under this fallen horse, I'll be saved tonight.' "

—Tom Malone

34. The Priest Who Can Save

In a restaurant a group of men at one of the tables were conversing upon the subject of religion. The argument grew so lively that it became impossible for those at the nearest tables not to hear it. As it proceeded, the interest of the listeners became intense.

The argument was chiefly as to whether salvation was by works or of grace, and whether a person could be assured of his salvation in this life. One of the disputants firmly insisted that salvation is, ". . . by grace . . . through faith; and that not of yourselves: it is the gift of God:" (Eph. 2:8).

Another contended that no man can know he is saved until he dies. As a final argument, he exclaimed, "Well, all I can say is this, I have placed myself in the hands of my priest, and he is responsible for my salvation."

At this point an elderly man rose from his table nearby and said, "Gentlemen, I believe I am known to you as a lawyer and a Christian. I could not help hearing the argument at your table, and I feel bound to say that our friend is perfectly logical in what he has said. I also have placed myself in the hands of my Priest, and He is responsible for my salvation. My priest is the Lord Jesus Christ. By faith I have committed myself into His hands, and 'I know whom I have believed, and am persuaded that he is able to keep that which I have committed unto him' " (II Tim. 1:12).

This settled the dispute. Such a statement from a man known to all for his high legal and Christian rating had an instant effect. Undoubtedly some men there heard the gospel for the first time as it was preached in a restaurant by an exponent of the law.

Let me ask you a question, Is your soul and its vast eternal concerns committed by precious faith to the One Great High Priest who never deceives or fails one who trusts Him? He is indeed responsible for the complete and perfect salvation, ". . . to the uttermost that come unto God by him" (Heb. 7:25).

—Selected

35. The Lancashire Girl Wanted Her Mother Saved

Some twenty years ago (1951) when I entered the gospel ministry I heard an illustration that gripped my heart. The illustration was told in a sermon which I heard Evangelist Fred Dillon preach. It was originally told by Charles H. Berry to J. H. Jowett.

In retelling the incident Dr. Jowett said:

"One night there came to me," Dr. Berry said, "a Lancashire girl, with her shawl over her head, and with clogs on her feet."

" 'Are you the minister?' she said.

" 'Yes.'

" 'Then I want you to come and get my mother in.'

"Thinking it was some drunken brawl, I said, 'You must get a policeman.'

" 'Oh, no,' said the girl, 'my mother is dying, and I want you to get her into salvation.'

" 'Where do you live?'

" 'I live so and so, a mile and a half from here.'

" 'Is there no minister nearer than I?'

" 'Oh, yes, but I want you, and you will have to come.'

"I was in my slippers. I did all I could to get out of it, but it was of no use. That girl was determined, and I had to dress and go. I found the house, and upstairs I found the poor woman dying. I sat down and talked about Jesus as the beautiful Example, and extolled Him as a Leader and Teacher. She looked at me out of her eyes of death, and said:

" 'Mister, that's no good for the likes of me. I don't want an example. I'm a sinner.'

"Jowett, there I was face to face with a poor soul dying, and had nothing to tell her. I had no gospel but I thought of what my mother had taught me, and I told her the old story of God's love in Christ's dying for sinful men, whether I believed or not.

" 'Now you are getting at it,' said the woman. 'That's the story for me.'

"So I got her in, and I got myself in. From that night," added Dr. Berry, "I have always had a full gospel of salvation for lost sinners."

Do you see now why this illustration has gripped my heart? While Dr. Berry got the Lancashire girl's mother in he got in himself. Do you know the Lord Jesus Christ as your personal Saviour?

The Lord Jesus said:

"For God so loved the world, that he gave his only begotten Son, that whosoever believeth in him should not perish, but have everlasting life" (John 3:16).

—Billy Apostolon

36. The Faith to Die in

Many years ago, in old London, a young Christian girl married a man who was an avowed atheist. She dearly loved him and hoped to win him to a belief in God, but her hopes were in vain. Later, when children began to come to them, he made a bargain with his wife. She was to be allowed a free hand in the religious training of any girls that might be born but he was to have complete control of any boys, and neither was to interfere with the other in religious matters.

The first child born to them was a boy, and the mother shuddered as she heard the father pour his blasphemous teachings into the childish ears. Later a little girl came to bless the home, and quite early in life the mother began to take the little one to Sunday School and church. The wee girlie learned the sweet hymns of childhood, such as "Jesus Loves Me" and often sang them to her brother. The parents' agreement did not bind the children, and the brother proved an apt pupil as his little sister told him the stories she learned in Sunday School of the Saviour who loves the children, and seeds of faith and love were sown in the little lad's heart.

One day, however, when the boy was about seven years of age, he was taken suddenly ill. The parents were stricken with grief when the physician said that there was but little hope of the boy's recovery. The father who except in the matter of religion, was a loving husband and a kind father, was as a man distracted, for his boy was as the apple of his eye.

He called the best physicians, and himself stayed by the boy's bedside day and night; but nothing could save his child. The little lad grew weaker, and one evening touched his Daddy's hand and said:

"Daddy, the doctor said I was going to die, didn't he?"

"Oh, my boy, don't talk like that! You must get better, Daddy can't spare you yet," sobbed the father.

"But, Daddy, I know I can't get better. I am going to die, and I want to ask you a question."

"What is it, my boy?"

"Daddy, whose faith shall I die in, yours or mother's?"

The grief stricken man turned his head from the child unable, or unwilling to answer. His religion was being tested to the full. Would it stand the test? Now was his chance to deny the existence of any hereafter. Surely there was nothing to be afraid of!

"Daddy, I'm dying. Whose faith shall I die in, yours or mother's?"

He who had boasted that there was no God, no Heaven and no Hell, dare not deceive his dying child, so he shouted with fierce earnestness:

"For God's sake, my boy, die in your mother's faith. Don't die in mine."

Unless your religion is good enough to commend to your children, whether for this present life or the life beyond, it is not worth having.

—T. DeCourcy Rayner

37. Jesus, the Way from Earth to Heaven

It is hard to believe that any human being could carry another person across the Niagara Falls on a tight rope stretched above the falls and for the two to live to tell the story. However, a Frenchman by the name of Charles Blondin actually did carry a man across on his shoulders walking on a rope stretched high above the thunderous falls. A vast throng saw him do this on August 19, 1859.

There were persons in the crowd that day who might have had their faith strengthened by the fact that on July 4, of the same year, Blondin crossed the falls blindfolded pushing a wheelbarrow before him. However, the unknown man on Blondin's shoulders was the only one who was actually carried across. Why were there no others taken across? The answer is that they did not commit themselves to the one person who could carry them in safety, and that man was Blondin, the Frenchman.

Here is an illustration of a great Bible truth. The Lord Jesus Christ is the only one who can carry individuals from earth to Heaven. The Apostle Peter declared: "Neither is there salvation in any other: for there is none other name under heaven given among men, whereby we must be saved" (Acts 4:12).

We see how it was necessary for that unknown man to commit himself absolutely to Blondin. Likewise, sinners must actually commit themselves to the Lord Jesus Christ depending upon Him alone to take them across the perilous Niagara of sin and eternal death.

Lift your heart to the Lord Jesus and say to Him, "Lord, I put my life into your hands. Save me from earth's darkened cliffs and prepare me for Heaven's shining shore."

—Author Unknown

38. The Young Lady Who Was Saved

from a Suicide's Death

Many years ago there lived in Dublin a beautiful and talented young lady, the wife of a young captain. At that time duelling was in vogue, and the captain having quarreled with O'Connell, the Irish Patriot, challenged him to a duel and was fatally wounded, and the young lady became a widow before she was eighteen.

First she tried solitude, and then the gayeties of life to rid herself of grief, but all in vain. One morning, early, she went down to a river to take her life. Just as she was about to take the fatal plunge she saw in a distant field a farmer plowing, calling to his horses and whistling cheerily as he followed the plow; and she said, bitterly, "Happy man! He has something to live for. He has a niche to fill." And there came to her a message as from God. "You have life, talents, opportunities. Why throw them away?" And turning from the river brink, she hurried home, saved from a suicide's death and doom.

Soon afterward, under a sermon on John 3:16, she was led to Christ, and several years after that married a Christian captain. Their son was Dr. Grattan Guinness. Not long before the death of Dr. Harry Guinness, he said, "If my honored father was used of God to turn thousands to Christ, if he was the means of training hundreds for the mission field; and if I, his son have done any service for God, then you must trace it back to that humble farmer doing his common task."

"The joy of the Lord is (our) strength." We never know what a Christian example is accomplishing.

—Scattered Seed

39. It Is What Christ Does That Counts

The wonderful violinist, Paganini, was one night in Paris playing before a great crowd. As he was tuning his violin, he broke one of the strings. The vast audience was disappointed. Paganini paid no attention, but put the instrument to his chin and began to play.

Soon another string snapped, and the audience frowned upon him. He went on, and by and by broke the third string, while his audience was grieved and maddened. Then quietly stepping to the front, he said, "Ladies and gentlemen," while he held up his violin, "one string and Paganini."

With that violin with but one string, he produced such music as had never before been heard. He made it sing like a nightingale, weep like a woman in distress; while the melody was as a chorus of angel voices. When he sat down the applause was wonderful. Women wept for joy and men shouted at the top of their voices.

One string and Paganini. That is it. Place yourself in the hand of the great Artist. Remembering that the music is in the Artist. The violin is only the instrument of its production.

You have been working, working, working, but with little results. Now cease your working and just let Christ work through you. Not the violin, but Paganini. Not I but Christ. You have been seeking power but not in the right way. Listen! It is not attainment but attitude that is power. It is not so much what you do for Christ but what you permit Him to do through you that counts. Be filled with the Spirit. Do you ask how? By yielding yourself to Him for his infilling and using.

—Oliver E. Williams

40. The Auction of Lady Anne Erskine's Soul

Rowland Hill, the great English preacher, was once speaking in a large auditorium. In the middle of his sermon, Lady Ann Erskine, who did not attend church often, but who was much in evidence at every prominent concert or ball, made an ostentatious entrance.

She had been heard previously to say that she would like sometime to hear Hill preach just "to please herself." Of course, when she entered the audience turned to see her in all her finery, the preacher recognized who she was.

All at once he stopped abruptly. "My friends," he shouted. "I have something here for sale." Everyone was startled. "I am going to auction something worth more than all the crowns of Europe—the soul of Lady Anne Erskine."

"Will anyone bid for her soul? Hark! I think I hear a bid. Who bids? *The World!*"

The lady's surprise was indescribable, as all eyes were now focused upon her.

"World, what will you give for her soul?"

"I will give pleasures, honor, and riches, a life of luxury and good times."

"Nothing more? Then your price is too small for us. For what would it profit the lady is she gained the whole world and lost her own soul? Hark! I hear another bid. Who bids? *Satan!*"

"I will give her the lust of the eyes, the lust of the flesh, and the pride of life. She can satisfy all her cravings with me."

"And what do you demand in return?" "Her soul! She passes once for all into my power."

"Your price is too high, Satan. You are a murderer from the beginning, a liar, and the father of lies. I can hear another bid. It is *the Lord Jesus Christ.*"

"I have already given My life for the lady. I have poured out My heart's blood for her when upon the cross I paid the ransom for the whole world. I will bring peace into her soul. I will clothe her with the garment of righteousness and adorn her with the gold of faith. I will keep her like a signet ring and take her to be with Myself in glory, for where I am there shall My servant be also."

"What dost Thou ask in return, Lord Jesus?"

"Her sin, her evil conscience, all that torments her."

"Lord Jesus, Thou shalt have her." Then turning to the lady he asked, "Lady Erskine, are you satisfied?"

"Yes," she answered with a loud, firm voice, while deep emotion passed through the whole meeting. Lady Erskine kept her word. From that hour her life was changed. She became a friend and mother to the poor and sick, the miserable and distressed. No one made so many sacrifices as she, for the cause of Jesus Christ. Throughout the remainder of her life she thanked God for the impulse that took her to hear Rowland Hill, and for the love that snatched her from the clutches of a deceiving world.

—G. D. Lemphers in *Moody Monthly*,
Copyrighted. Used by permission.

41. The Fear of Death Gripped the Man's Heart

A Christian young lady in London, England, had an unsaved uncle. She wanted to win him to the Lord. She had begged him, like many Christians beg their friends, loved ones, and neighbors to go to church. She had begged him to go to church with her on a certain Sunday night and he finally consented.

That night the young lady prayed, "Now Lord, my unsaved uncle, for whom I have prayed and wept for so many times, is going to be in the service tonight. Dear Lord, may there be an evangelistic, soul-saving message preached tonight that will bring him to Christ."

As the young lady sat by the side of her uncle praying, the preacher that night said, "I am reading to you tonight from Genesis 5." He read eight times in that chapter this expression, ". . . and he died . . . and he died . . . and he died."

The young lady testified, "I was almost disappointed for I said to myself what is there in that chapter that can lead my uncle to a saving knowledge of Jesus Christ?"

The service closed and he was not saved. They walked along the sidewalk of London that night, and she wept as she walked because she thought her prayer had not been answered.

In the wee hours of that night, the young lady's phone rang and her uncle said, "I want you to come and tell me how to be saved. Something the preacher read from the Bible tonight has gripped my heart. I have heard it ten thousand times since he read it."

She said, "What is it uncle?"

Over the phone, he said, "That expression, '. . . and he died . . . and he died . . . and he died.' has gone back and forth through my mind thousands of times. I have been made to face death. I have had brought to me the reality of death for myself and I must be saved."

—Tom Malone

42. When Opportunity Knocked at Gene Autry's Door

When I was a boy, I liked Saturday to come. I lived on a farm with my father, George Apostolon and my brother Demetris. My mother had died when I was only four years of age. My father, a restaurant operator, was advised by Dr. R. G. Broadus to take my brother out on a farm where he could have a healthy environment and gain strength from a serious illness which he had previously experienced. This my father did.

When Saturday came my father would go to town to buy groceries and my brother and I would go with him and would go to see a cowboy western. One of our favorites was Gene Autry.

In 1925, when Gene Autry was only 17, he was working as a telegraph operator for the Oklahoma railroad. One July night he was picking his mail order guitar and singing to himself while one lone customer was writing a telegram.

After the stranger finished writing he wanted Gene to play him another song, and after that another. After listening, the stranger said, "Young fellow, you've got a lot to learn, but you're pretty good. You're wasting your time here. You ought to quit and try radio.

After the courteous visitor left Gene looked at the man's signature and he was stunned as he realized that the person who advised him was Will Rogers, then the most popular humorist in America.

Gene quit his job within two weeks, went to Tulsa, got a job with station KVOO, later became "Oklahoma's Yodeling Cowboy" and continued until he became the nation's most outstanding western entertainer.

When opportunity knocked at Gene Autry's door, he opened the door. Opportunity is now knocking at your door.

The Lord Jesus said:

> "Behold, I stand at the door, and knock: if any man hear my voice, and open the door, I will come in to him, and will sup with him, and he with me" (Rev. 3:20).

Will you open the door of your heart and let the Lord Jesus in?

—Billy Apostolon

43. Christ Died So That We Could Live

A young soldier had been brought up on trial and condemned to death. He had been guilty of treason, and condemned by the judges to die, when up stepped his older brother, who had served in his country's wars, and had both his arms cut off. This brother, standing before the judges, holding up the stumps of his arms, pleaded for his brother's life; not for what his brother had done, but for what he had done.

He confessed that his brother was guilty. He confessed that his brother was worthy of death; but for what he had done in the service of his country, he pleaded that his brother's life might be spared. Looking on what the brother had done, the judges for his sake pardoned the guilty brother.

Ah! That is just what the Lord Jesus Christ does for us sinners. Christ suffered and died on Calvary's cross that we might live. We deserve death and eternal condemnation, but in the presence of God is the Lord Jesus Christ whose hands and feet are scarred by nails, whose side is marked by a sword. These tell the everlasting story of sins which were borne by Him in love, and now, if any will accept Him as their Saviour, and put their trust in Him, they are forgiven.

God pardons our sins for the sake of Christ, because He laid down His life that we might live.

Can you truly say with the poet in the expression of his heart and the confession of his faith:

> "In peace let me resign my breath,
>   And Thy salvation see;
> My sins deserve eternal death,
>   But Jesus died for me."

"But he was wounded for our transgressions, he was bruised for our iniquities: the chastisement of our peace was upon him; and with his stripes we are healed" (Isa. 53:5).

"Who his own self bare our sins in his own body on the tree, that we, being dead to sins, should live unto righteousness: by whose stripes ye were healed" (I Peter 2:24).

—Author Unknown

44. A New Coat for an Old Blanket

An Indian and a white man, at a gospel meeting together, were both brought under conviction of sin by the same sermon. The Indian shortly thereafter received Christ as his Saviour and was led to rejoice in pardoning mercy. The white man for a long time was under great distress of mind, and at times was ready to despair. At last he too was brought to see the way and to rejoice in the forgiveness of his sins.

Some time afterwards, meeting his red brother, the white man said, "How is it, brother, that I should be so long under conviction of sin, while you found comfort so soon?"

"Oh, brother," replied the Indian, "me tell you. There come along a rich prince. He propose to give you a new coat. You look at your coat, and say, 'I don't know. My coat pretty good. I think it will do a little longer.'

"The rich man then offer me new coat. I look at my old blanket. I say, 'This rag good for nothing.' I fling my blanket away and take the new coat. Just so, brother, you try to keep your own righteousness for some time. You think it good. You don't like to give it up! But I, poor Indian, had nothing. I glad at once to receive the Lord Jesus Christ as my righteousness."

Sinner, are you like the white man, trying to hold on to some fancied goodness in yourself? Have you not discovered that what God says of you is true?

> "But we are all as an unclean thing, and all our righteousnesses are as filthy rags . . . " (Isa. 64:6a).
> "For all have sinned, and come short of the glory of God" (Rom. 3:23).

Throw away the old blanket of your own righteousness. It isn't fit for the holy presence of God. Take Christ, and you will then be able to sing:

> "Clad in this robe, how bright I shine!
> Angels possess not such a dress;
> Angels have not a robe like mine—
> Jesus the Lord is my righteousness."

—Echoes of Grace

45. The Peace That Christ Bids

There is to be found nowhere a finer illustration of peace in the Christian life than was manifested in President Mc Kinley. On the last afternoon of his life he began to realize that his life was slipping away. He called his surgeons to his bedside and said:

"It is useless, gentlemen. I think we ought to have prayer."

The dying man crossed his hands on his chest and closed his eyes.

He prayed, "Our Father which art in Heaven."

The lips of the surgeons moved. "Hallowed be thy name. Thy kingdom come, thy will be done."

The quietness was broken by the sobbing of a nurse.

"Thy will be done on earth as it is in Heaven."

The sands of life were running swiftly.

"Give us this day our daily bread; and forgive us our debts

as we forgive our debtors; and lead us not into temptation but deliver us from evil."

There was a brief silence. The surgeons looked at the trembling lips.

"For thine is the kingdom, the power, and the glory, forever, Amen."

"Amen," whispered the surgeons.

A little later he called for his wife. She came in, sat down by his bedside, took his hands in hers and kissed them. As he felt the touch of her lips he faintly smiled and said, "Good-bye! Goodbye, all! It is God's way. His will, not ours, be done."

Such is the peace that Christ bids.

—H. M. Woods

46. She Lost a Golden Opportunity

Mrs. Barney, the prison worker, went to a western city to speak. She was met at the railway station by a lady who was to entertain her. She went to the home of her hostess in an old rattletrap carriage driven by a rednosed young man. When Mrs. Barney stepped inside the door of the home, her hostess apologized for the appearance of the carriage and the driver, explaining that she did not feel free to employ any other, and said, "O, Mrs. Barney, will you kneel here with me and pray for that driver?"

After the prayer she told Mrs. Barney the story. Several years before she had been given a class of five boys in the Sunday School of her church. These boys had been gathered from the streets. She thought it her duty to entertain the boys by telling them stories during the lesson hour, and when the matter of their personal salvation would be pressed home on her she would say, "Oh, that isn't my business, that's the pastor's work."

After a time she moved to another city and was compelled to give up her class. During her residence in that city she came to a new vision of Christ. Then she began to realize that she had lost a golden opportunity in that she had neglected to teach the Bible in such a way as to lead those boys to a personal knowledge of Christ.

Five years afterward she returned to the city and inquired for her boys. No one in the church knew anything about them. One day she found this young man driving a cab, and he was under the influence of liquor. When she asked him about the other boys, he said, "Oh, lady, two of us are dead, and two of us are in prison, and I'm the only one left!" She begged him to become a Christian, but he said, "No, lady. There was a time when I would have done anything for you, but it's too late now—too late now." She had lost her opportunity.

—The Pastor His Own Evangelist

47. Captured by His Conscience

The biblical warning, "Be sure your sin will find you out" (Num. 32:23), is fulfilled in many different ways. Years ago an honor camp inmate of San Quentin prison in California, created a national sensation when he and three other inmates escaped by plane.

The honor inmate would have been eligible for parole in a few months. However, he escaped with his three companions to Medford, Oregon. His three companions were almost immediately recaptured. That was in 1956. He left Medford and went on to Butte, Montana, married, and his wife later was expecting a child.

He did not get caught in his sin—*publicly*! However, his sin found him out privately to the extent that he was "*afraid to look at myself in the mirror,*" as he himself later testified.

The escapee, under conviction, accompanied by his father and his lawyer, returned to San Quentin and surrendered to the warden with the explanation that he wanted "*To start a new life without being afraid to look at myself in the mirror.*" His conscience had "captured" him!

—Robert L. Sumner
Evangelist, former pastor of Temple Baptist
Church in Portsmouth, Ohio.

48. How a Skeptic Was Saved

When Horace Bushnell was at Yale College as a tutor, he was skeptical, and his influence on the students was harmful. He felt this burden of responsibility somewhat himself, and, as he afterwards expressed it to a friend, he said that he thought he was "like a great snag in the river that caught the shipping as it came down, and held it fast."

He could not bear this responsibility, so one night he sat down in his study to take stock of what he really did believe. He concluded that he knew two things. First, that God was God, and second, that right was right; although he did not believe in the divinity of Christ, nor in the inspiration of the Bible.

The thought occurred to him, "What is the use of my trying to get further knowledge, so long as I do not cheerfully yield myself to do that which has already been revealed to me?"

Moved by this thought, he knelt down and prayed a prayer something like this: "Oh, God!" he said, "I believe there is an ineradicable, eternal distinction between right and wrong, and I hereby give myself up to do the right and to refrain from doing the wrong; and I believe that thou dost exist, and if thou canst hear my cry and wilt reveal thyself unto me I pledge myself that I will do thy will, and I make this pledge fully and freely and forever."

God took him by the hand and lifted him up and led him where he gained a magnificent conception of Jesus Christ, and found salvation for himself and others.

—Mills

49. Rich beyond All Comparison

One day William Reynolds, a Sunday School Missionary, went to see an old man in Illinois, who boasted of being an infidel. The people told Mr. Reynolds not to speak to him about his soul because it would make him very angry.

The old man asked Mr. Reynolds to go up with him into the cupola of his barn and look at his great farm. When they got up there, he said, "Mr. Reynolds, I came out here a poor boy when I was eighteen and I didn't own a cent, and now I own everything you can see in every direction. Do you see those big fields of waving grain? Do you see those great pastures and meadowlands? Do you see the great stretch of woodland? Do you see those great herds of cattle and droves of sheep?"

"They are all mine!" said the old infidel, as he pointed in the four directions of the compass.

"Well," said Mr. Reynolds, "You are a pretty rich man in all those directions, but how much do you own in that direction?" pointing toward Heaven.

The rich old farmer looked up, and then he dropped his head on his breast and said, "I guess I don't own very much in that direction."

> "For what shall it profit a man, if he shall gain the whole world and lose his own soul?" (Mark 8:36).

Heaven pity you if you are unsaved, you are a pauper in the sight of God! However, the man who has trusted fully in Christ's finished work on Calvary for his salvation is rich beyond all comparison.

> "For God so loved the world, that he gave his only begotten Son, that whosoever believeth in him should not perish, but have everlasting life" (John 3:16).

—Selected

50. Drifting into the Jaws of Death

Years ago at Niagara Falls, a young man was employed as a guide. Having nothing to do one day, he moored his boat well above the cataract and lay down in it to rest. Rocked on the bosom of the ever-moving waters, he fell asleep. He thought he had tied the boat securely, but with its constant swaying it was finally loosed, and with its unconscious occupant, began to drift with the current. Spectators on the shore, seeing his grave danger, shouted loudly to awaken him, that he might save himself while as yet the current was not rapid, but to no purpose.

At one point in the boat's progress it was grounded upon a rock that protruded in midstream. Seeing the pause, the bystanders redoubled their efforts to arouse the sleeping man, crying lustily to him, "Get on the rock! Get on the rock!" But he slumbered on, oblivious to his extreme peril.

With the movement of the waters the boat was soon cleared from the rock, and heading for the falls. The poor man was aroused from his sleep only amidst the thundering roar of the great cataract, over which he plunged to his death.

How appalling! Asleep in the boat! Calmly and unconsciously drifting into the very jaws of death! One trembles to think of it.

Yet how aptly this illustrates the indifference of souls today! Many unconcerned as to their fatal course, fast asleep in their sins, perhaps lulled on the tide by earthly pleasures, soothed into false confidence by their dependence on a blameless life or religious profession. *All asleep in the boat!*

> ". . . the god of this world hath blinded the minds of them which believe not, lest the light of the glorious gospel of Christ, who is the image of God, should shine unto them" (II Cor. 4:4).

Are you safely moored to the Rock, or are you drifting with the tide? Have you Christ as your Saviour, or are you carried along with the broad, rapid current of a world that is fast approaching its destruction. If still unsaved, will you not awake to the danger of going on without Christ? If you keep putting off the salvation of your soul till some future day, you may suddenly wake up too late and find yourself taking that last fatal plunge over the brink into the dark waters of death and the fearful woes of a lost eternity.

"... Awake thou that sleepest ..." (Eph. 5:14).
"... Believe on the Lord Jesus Christ, and thou shalt be saved ..." (Acts 16:31).

—The Exalter

51. The Convict Was under Spiritual Arrest

Disquieting news was abroad. A convict had escaped from the penitentiary, and although the machinery of the law had been set in motion, no trace of him could be found.

At the time, French Oliver, the noted preacher, was conducting a mission in the neighborhood of that prison. Night after night he pleaded passionately with men and women to come to Christ, and for several consecutive nights he noticed a man who invariably sat near the rear of the hall. There was an intense light in his eyes indicating his earnest interest, and the drawn, haggard expression on his face told of the soul agony within.

At last one night Dr. Oliver felt constrained to speak to the listener. He left the platform, and going straight to the man said, "Why on earth don't you surrender to Christ?"

The words bursting from him, the man said, "I have been in Hell the last four days, sir. I am under *spiritual arrest!* I would have escaped from here, but I just couldn't."

Looking intently at Dr. Oliver, he said, "I judge you know who I am. I am the man they are hunting for! If I surrender to Christ, it means the penitentiary again for me."

As the convict spoke he shuddered. Dr. Oliver said to him, "The question for you to settle tonight is God's penitentiary, not man's. It is impossible for you to escape the Private Detective of God Almighty—the Holy Spirit."

The man fell on his knees sobbing. The flood tide of God's love in Christ crashed through the rebellion of his sin-scarred heart and he surrendered to the Saviour.

He went back to the penitentiary of his own accord and there he told the warden of his conversion to Christ. The warden, looking him in the face, said, "Man, I know you, and nothing but God Almighty could have made you come back here."

Once again the gates of the prison closed on him, and he finished his sentence, leaving an unblemished record from the time of his return. At the conclusion of his sentence a position was found for him, and he became a strong witness to the saving power of Christ, the Son of God.

Have you realized that you are under arrest? More than that, you are condemned and sentenced. By whom? By God Almighty!

> "He that believeth on him is not condemned: but he that believeth not is condemned already, because he hath not believed in the name of the only begotten Son of God" (John 3:18).
>
> —Echoes of Grace

52. The Operator Dialed the Right Number

A young woman came before the session of a Presbyterian church and said that she wished to unite with that church. No one present knew her. She made an unusually clear confession of faith, impressing the minister so much that he asked her how she had been led to Christ.

"Through Dr. S-------," she replied.

"Is Dr. S-------, a friend of yours?" she was asked.

"No," she said, "I have never met or even seen him."

She was a telephone operator, and had had night service, from 9 p.m. to 3 a.m. Receiving many calls for this physician, Dr. S-------, she had more than once rung his bell by mistake. Always he answered, not only with courtesy, but in a voice that showed no trace of impatience. It was such a grateful relief from the surly, sleepy voices of others awakened at midnight or the harsh expressions directed at her when she called a wrong number by mistake, that she finally became deeply interested and wanted to know the secret of the difference between Dr. S-------, and other men.

She made inquiries about him, until she learned that Christ was supreme in his heart and life, and that what she was so admiring in him was simply Christ living in an earnest Christian. Soon Dr. S-------'s Saviour was her Saviour.

"I am the door: by me if any man enter in, he shall be saved, and shall go in and out, and find pasture" (John 10:9).

—Selected